Gases

Charlotte Deschermeier

PowerKiDS press™

New York

Published in 2014 by The Rosen Publishing Group, Inc.
29 East 21st Street, New York, NY 1001 0

Photo Credits: © 2003-2013 Shutterstock, Inc.

Library of Congress Cataloging-in-Publication Data

Deschermeier, Charlotte, author.
 Gases / by Charlotte Deschermeier.
    pages cm. – (Ultimate science. Physical science)
 Includes index.
 ISBN 978-1-4777-6081-9 (library) – ISBN 978-1-4777-6082-6 (pbk.) –
 ISBN 978-1-4777-6083-3 (6-pack)
 1. Gases–Juvenile literature. 2. Matter–Properties–Juvenile literature. I. Title.
 QC161.2.D47 2014
 530.4'3–dc23
                                    2013023459

Manufactured in the United States of America

CPSIA Compliance Information: Batch #W14PK4: For Further Information contact Rosen Publishing, New York, New York at 1-800-237-9932

Contents

Matter on the Move   4

Gases and Fluidity   6

Gases and Volume   8

Gases and Shape   10

Gases and Expansion   12

Gases and Compressibility   14

Density and Temperature   16

Important Oxygen   18

Nitrogen and Hydrogen   20

Gases are Everywhere   22

Glossary   23

Index   24

Websites   24

Matter on the Move

Do you know what a toad, the air you breathe, and a glass of milk have in common? They are all made of matter. Matter exists in different states. On Earth, the three most common states are solids, liquids, and gases. You cannot always see, smell, or feel gases. However, they are all around you. All matter, including gases, is made of tiny pieces called molecules. Molecules are made up of one or more **atoms**. A molecule of **oxygen** gas, for example, is made of two oxygen atoms.

We can recognize gases on the basis of many special **properties** that they have.

Molecules of methane gas, shown here, are formed by one carbon atom and four hydrogen atoms. Methane gas in the air helps trap the heat of the Sun.

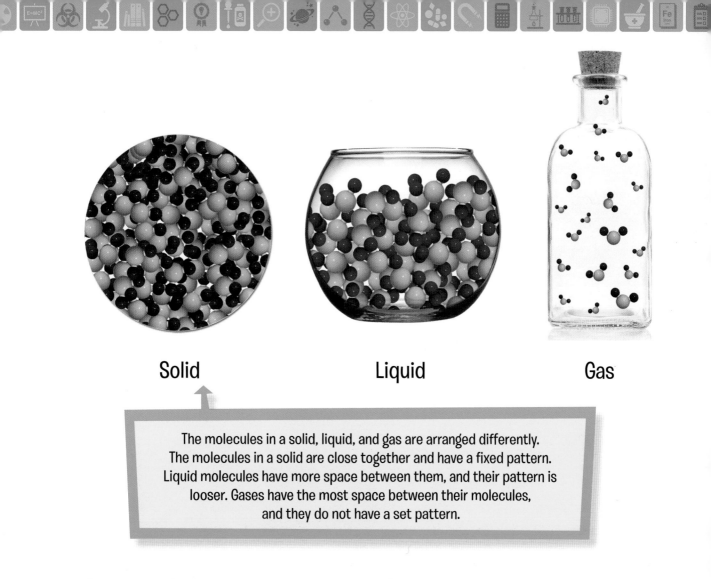

Solid   Liquid   Gas

The molecules in a solid, liquid, and gas are arranged differently. The molecules in a solid are close together and have a fixed pattern. Liquid molecules have more space between them, and their pattern is looser. Gases have the most space between their molecules, and they do not have a set pattern.

Gas molecules are constantly in motion. As they move, they **bounce** off each other and objects around them. This movement does not change the gas molecule. The gas molecule does not slow down or stick to other gas molecules or to objects. It just never stops moving.

Gases and Fluidity

The molecules that make up matter are held together by bonds, or intermolecular forces. Molecules that are close together have strong intermolecular forces. For example, the molecules in a solid are packed tightly together. There is not much molecular movement.

The air around Earth is filled with gases. This blanket of gases is called the atmosphere.

Intermolecular forces between molecules that are far apart are weak. The molecules in a gas have a lot of space between them.

Gas molecules are small and move quickly. As gas molecules move and bounce off each other, they spread out and fill whatever **container** they are placed in. In fact, gases will spread out as far as they can. The movement of molecules is called fluidity. Fluidity is what allows something to flow.

This is a model of an oxygen molecule. One molecule of oxygen is made up of two oxygen atoms. They are held together by bonds.

Gases and Volume

Volume is the amount of space that a **substance** takes up. Gases do not have a set volume. Molecules in a gas move and fill up the volume of the container in which they are placed.

If a gas in a small container is put into a larger container, the gas molecules will spread out. As they fill the larger volume, they will have greater space between them.

This glass tube is filled with air. If the tube had a lid, the gas would spread out and completely fill the container. Because the tube is open, the gas fills the container and spreads out to fill the surrounding space, too.

These balloons are filled with helium. The helium takes on the shape of the balloon that it fills. If the helium were moved from a small balloon into a larger balloon, it would spread out to fill the new space. Helium is a light gas. It allows the balloons to float in the air.

For example, suppose you went to a circus and bought a balloon filled with helium gas. The helium molecules inside the balloon are moving quickly. They are bouncing off each other and the sides of the balloon. If you pop the balloon in your bedroom, the helium molecules will move and spread out into your whole room. Soon they will be bouncing off the walls as they fill the entire volume of the room. Inside the balloon, the helium molecules were closer than they will be in your room.

Gases and Shape

Matter gets its shape from the arrangement of molecules. For example, the shape of a solid is created by the pattern of its tightly packed molecules. The molecules of a gas are not arranged in a pattern. Therefore gas has no shape of its own. Instead it moves to take the shape of whatever is holding it.

For example, there are metal tanks that hold oxygen gas for people to breathe when they swim underwater for a long time. They are shaped like a **cylinder**. The oxygen gas moves around in the tank and takes the same cylindrical shape of the tank.

This beach ball is filled with air. If you open the stopper on the ball and push the air out, that air will no longer hold the round shape of the ball.

If you blow up a round beach ball with air, the air will take on a round shape too. The shape of the gas inside each object is the same shape as the object itself.

If the object holding a gas changes shape, the gas inside it also changes shape. For example, suppose you pull on the ends of a round, fat balloon to make it a long, thin balloon. The gas inside will then take the shape of the balloon.

People need air to breathe. There is no air underwater. However, because gases will fill whatever container they are placed in, we can bring air with us underwater. This diver has an air tank on his back. This lets him breathe as he studies the living things and their surroundings in the ocean.

Gases and Expansion

Gas expands, or takes up more volume, as gas molecules move farther and farther apart. Over time a gas will completely fill the space it is in. If the gas is in a closed container, the molecules expand until they are stopped by the walls of the container. If the gas is in an open container, the gas molecules expand out of the container and become part of the air surrounding them.

The movement of gas molecules from one area to another is called diffusion. Our sense of smell is one way in which we **experience** diffusion.

This glass tube has a gas called bromine in it. Because bromine has a color, you can see diffusion in action.

When a bottle of perfume is opened at one end of a room, eventually the smell will spread to the other side of the room. The room has become the gas's container. Diffusion occurred as the perfume molecules mixed with the room's air and spread throughout the room.

Natural gas is found in the soil after living things break down under pressure. This gas is used as a fuel for such things as heating our homes and cooking food. Natural gas has no smell, color, or taste. However, people add a smell to natural gas so we will know when it is spreading out, or diffusing, into the air.

Gases and Compressibility

A gas will compress, or become smaller, if it is forced into a smaller container. With less room in which to move, the gas molecules are forced closer together. They **squeeze** into the empty spaces that once existed between them.

You compress gas when you pump your bike tires with air. Many gas molecules are squeezed into the tire's small space, as air is forced into the tire.

A bike tire is filled with compressed air. The more air you pump into the tire, the firmer the tire becomes. If you put only a little air into the tire, the air would spread out to fill the tire, but the tire would be too soft to use.

As long as a gas stays in a small container, it will stay compressed. If the container gets bigger, the gas molecules begin to move apart, and the gas expands. Have you ever heard a whooshing sound when you opened a can of soda? That sound is made by a gas called carbon dioxide. It makes that noise because the compressed gas inside the soda expands.

Aerosol cans work because a liquid and a gas are compressed inside the can. When the button on top of the can is pressed, it opens a small hole. The gas inside the can expands and moves out of the can. This forces the liquid out in a fine mist.

Density and Temperature

The amount of matter in a certain volume is called density. It tells you how closely packed the molecules in a substance are. The closer the molecules of a substance are to each other, the greater its density. The molecules of gases are usually loosely packed, with empty spaces between them. Gases are usually less dense than solids and liquids. Changing **temperatures** can change how molecules move in a gas. At high temperatures the gas molecules move faster and spread farther apart. The gas's volume increases by this.

Weather is created when temperatures go up or down and the gases in the air crash into each other with greater or lesser force. This causes high-pressure or low-pressure areas. We use a tool called a barometer, shown here, to measure air pressure.

The molecules of a gas slow down and move closer together when the temperature is lowered. The volume of a gas becomes smaller in colder temperatures.

When gas molecules collide, **pressure** is created. Increasing the temperature of a gas will increase its pressure. The molecules will collide with one another and the sides of their container with greater force. Lowering the temperature of a gas causes the molecules to slow down because of its lower pressure.

Dry ice does not melt into a liquid. Instead it changes directly into carbon dioxide gas, which sinks toward the ground. The gas sinks because the carbon dioxide gas is denser than the air.

Important Oxygen

Can you think of a gas that is needed by people, animals, and all living things to live? The answer is oxygen. This gas is colorless, tasteless, and odorless. Oxygen makes up almost 21 **percent** of Earth's **atmosphere**. Trees, bushes, grasses, and other plants create most of Earth's oxygen during **photosynthesis**. During photosynthesis, plants take in a gas called carbon dioxide through their leaves. Carbon dioxide, sunshine, and water are used by plants to make their food and oxygen.

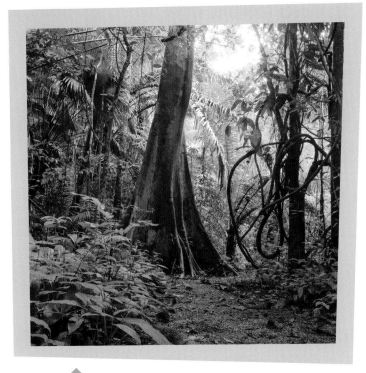

A rain forest is a large, wet area filled with plants and animals. Rain forests once covered 14 percent of Earth. Today they cover only about 7 percent of Earth. Because rain forests are being cut down, we are losing many of the plants that produce the oxygen we need to live.

To breathe, people and animals take in oxygen. Once oxygen is inside the body, the blood then carries it to every cell in the body. The body uses the oxygen to make **energy**.

Oxygen is a part of most solids. Solid oxygen makes up about 46 percent of Earth's **crust**. Oxygen gas can also be made into a liquid. Liquid oxygen is added to some **fuels** because it helps the fuel burn faster. This makes liquid oxygen useful in rocket fuel. Rocket fuel is used in the engines of spacecraft, such as the space shuttle. Blasting off takes up a huge amount of energy.

The space shuttle uses fuel that includes liquid oxygen and hydrogen. This fuel gives the shuttle the power it needs to exit Earth's atmosphere and enter space.

gen and Hydrogen

xygen, other gases are needed for life on Earth. Nitrogen gas
ut 78 percent of the air around you. Nitrogen gas has no color,
. It is nonflammable, which means that it will not burn. Nitrogen
usually combine with other gases or elements.

he most plentiful gas in the universe. The universe is all of space.
he lightest known gas. It has no color, no odor, and no taste.
ns easily, making it flammable.

The universe is filled with gases, including hydrogen. The Sun's atmosphere is made mostly of hydrogen.

It is almost impossible to find hydrogen alone as a gas. Instead it combines with other elements to form **compounds**.

Did you know that hydrogen combines with another gas to make water? Water is a liquid made from oxygen and hydrogen. Water is quite an important substance. It covers around three-quarters of Earth's surface. All living things depend on it to live. The next time you go swimming, be sure to think about the gases that are making it possible.

Hydrogen combined with carbon can create a compound known as propane. Propane is used in many gas grills. Summer barbecues would not be the same without hydrogen gas!

Gases are Everywhere

The Earth is surrounded by a large blanket made of gases. This blanket of gases is called the atmosphere. The atmosphere reaches hundreds of miles (km) above Earth. In addition to oxygen and nitrogen, gases such as argon, methane, and carbon dioxide are found in Earth's atmosphere. Water vapor, the gaseous form of water, is also in our atmosphere. The gases in our atmosphere keep Earth safe from the harmful rays of the Sun. At the same time, the gases also prevent Earth from getting too cold. They trap the warmth of the Sun's rays that have reached Earth. Without gases we could not breathe. We also would not have the important compounds, such as water, on which we depend.

We cannot see them, feel them, or smell them, but gases surround us. We depend on gases and their properties every day. Without them our world would be completely different.

Glossary

atmosphere (AT-muh-sfeer) The gases around an object in space. On Earth, this is air.

atoms (A-temz) The smallest parts of elements that can exist either alone or with other elements.

bounce (BOWNS) To spring up, down, or to the side.

compounds (KOM-powndz) Two or more things combined.

container (kun-TAY-ner) Something that holds things.

crust (KRUST) The outer, or top, layer of a planet.

cylinder (SIH-len-der) A tubelike object.

energy (EH-nur-jee) The power to work or to act.

experience (ik-SPEER-ee-ents) To learn by taking part or seeing for oneself.

fuels (FYOOLZ) Things used to make energy, warmth, or power.

oxygen (OK-sih-jen) A gas that has no color, taste, or odor and is necessary for people and animals to breathe.

percent (pur-SENT) One part of 100.

photosynthesis (foh-toh-SIN-thuh-sus) The way in which green plants make their own food from sunlight, water, and a gas called carbon dioxide.

pressure (PREH-shur) A force that pushes on something.

properties (PRAH-pur-teez) Features that belong to something.

squeeze (SKWEEZ) To crowd into a limited area.

substance (SUB-stans) Matter that takes up space.

temperatures (TEM-pur-cherz) How hot or cold things are.

Index

A
atmosphere, 18, 22
atoms, 4

C
carbon dioxide, 15, 18, 22

D
density, 16
diffusion, 12-13

F
fluidity, 7

H
helium, 9
hydrogen, 20-21

I
intermolecular forces, 6-7

M
molecule(s), 4-10, 12-17

N
nitrogen, 20, 22

O
oxygen, 4, 10, 18-22

P
photosynthesis, 18
pressure, 17

T
temperature(s), 16-17

V
volume, 8-9, 12, 16-17

Websites

Due to the changing nature of Internet links, PowerKids Press has developed an online list of websites related to the subject of this book. This site is updated regularly. Please use this link to access the list:

www.powerkidslinks.com/usps/gases/